YOU MUST **1943** THIS

2001

MILESTONES, MEMORIES, TRIVIA AND FACTS, NEWS EVENTS, PROMINENT PERSONALITIES & SPORTS HIGHLIGHTS OF THE YEAR

TO : *Allen*

FROM : *Twyla* ♡

MESSAGE : *HAppy   58 years*

selected and researched
by
betsy dexter

WARNER ⓦ TREASURES™

PUBLISHED BY WARNER BOOKS

A TIME WARNER COMPANY

Warner Books, Inc.
1271 Avenue of the Americas
New York, New York 10020

Warner Treasures is a
trademark of Warner Books, Inc.

A Time Warner Company

CAROL BOKUNIEWICZ DESIGN
PRINTED IN SINGAPORE
FIRST PRINTING : SEPTEMBER 1995
10 9 8 7 6 5 4 3 2 1
ISBN : 0-446-91076-7

President Roosevelt, in his third term, attended war conferences with Prime Minister Winston Churchill in Casablanca and Quebec, with Churchill and Soviet Premier Josef Stalin in Teheran, with Churchill and Chinese leader Chiang Kai-shek in Cairo. On one thing they all agreed—to demand unconditional surrender from the Axis powers.

Under **Dwight D. Eisenhower**, commander in chief of Allied forces in Africa, the U.S. captured Bizerte, Tunisia, and drove Axis forces out of Africa.

At the Battle of Bismarck Sea, U.S. bombers sank a Japanese convoy of 22 ships.

President Roosevelt named General Dwight D. Eisenhower Supreme Commander of the Allied Expeditionary Force, planning an invasion of Western Europe.

The 7th Army, under **General George S. Patton**, conquered Sicily. U.S. forces landed south of Naples and pushed back German and Italian defenses.

BURMA DECLARED WAR ON THE UNITED STATES.

newsreel

On August 3, **John Fitzgerald Kennedy**, son of the ex-ambassador to Great Britain, saved his crew after a Japanese destroyer split it in two. He and the crew were rescued on August 7.

U.S. naval and amphibious divisions began island-hopping in the Pacific, capturing enough key bases to force the Japanese to retreat on New Guinea.

1943

3

King Victor Emmanuel III of Italy placed **Premier Benito Mussolini** under arrest. The Italian government, under new premier Pietro Badoglio, surrendered and joined the Allies.

After a 17-month siege, the Soviet Army rescued Leningrad. The German 6th Army surrendered.

The Allies began round-the-clock bombing of German cities, concentrating on munitions and aircraft plants in the heavily industrial Ruhr Valley.

Led by Marshal Josef Tito, Yugoslav guerillas battled German occupation troops near Trieste.

headlines

international

An accident in a London bomb shelter killed 178 people, mostly women and children, when a little boy tripped on the stairs, causing others to pile up behind and suffocate.

Iran declared war on Germany and joined the Allies.

In a startling reversal of policy, the Soviet Union announced that Communist parties in other nations would be granted nominal autonomy. Stalinism was still the model for these other Communist countries.

Chiang Kai-shek became president
of the Chinese Nationalist Republic.

OKLAHOMA!

This year saw the first collaboration between composer Richard Rodgers and lyricist Oscar Hammerstein, II. Their Broadway debut kicked off with the enormously successful **Oklahoma!**, featuring the song "Oh What a Beautiful Morning" and choreography by Agnes de Mille.

"Big Inch," the world's longest oil pipeline, was dedicated. It extended 1,300 miles, from Texas to Pennsylvania.

U.S. Army engineers completed the Pentagon building, the headquarters of the Department of Defense, which remains one of the largest office buildings on the planet.

Reflecting the tumult of world events, it was a year of upheaval for the art world. **Jackson Pollock's** work was shown for the first time in November at Peggy Guggenheim's Manhattan art museum, where reaction varied from "genius" to "junk." **Picasso** completed *The Bull's Head*, considered by some to be the first found-object sculpture. Painter **Robert Motherwell** took abstract expressionism in an entirely new direction with his most famous work, *Pancho Villa, Dead and Alive*.

On February 7, **rationing** of canned food began. Coupon books were issued for processed foods on March 1. By government order, beginning March 29, sale of butter, fat, lard, and oils was halted for a week.

cultural
milestones

On April 13, the Jefferson Memorial was dedicated in Washington, DC.

In England, a parliamentary ruling declared that women no longer had to wear hats in court.

An infantile paralysis (polio) epidemic killed 1,792 persons between January and September, and crippled thousands.

BOB HOPE

radio

On **perry mason** (CBS Radio), Erle Stanley Gardner's literary sleuth turned up as a foppish playboy in a sudsy daytime serial starring Bartlett Robinson.

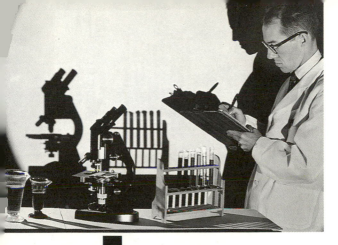

science

Large-scale production of **penicillin** began to meet the demand as the drug was used to treat a variety of infectious diseases.

Zenith radio introduced a $40 hearing aid. Previously hearing aids could only be found for $150–$200.

Henry Kaiser developed a technique of prefabrication allowing him to build a 100,000-ton *Liberty* ship in 4 days.

Swiss chemist Albert Hoffman accidentally ingested LSD, discovering the drug's bizarre hallucinogenic powers— and experiencing the world's first "bad trip."

milestones

celeb births

FABIAN, fifties teen idol, on February 6, in Philadelphia.

JOE PESCI, actor, in Newark, NJ, on February 9.

GEORGE HARRISON, Beatle, in Liverpool, England, on February 25.

LYNN REDGRAVE, actress, March 8, in London.

GEORGE BENSON, guitarist and singer, Pittsburgh, PA, on March 22.

CHRISTOPHER WALKEN, actor, in New York, on March 31.

MICHAEL PALIN, actor and cofounder of "Monty Python's Flying Circus," in London, on May 5.

TONI TENILLE, half of duo The Captain and Tenille, in Montgomery, AL, on May 8.

LESLIE UGGAMS, singer, in New York, on May 25.

MALCOLM MCDOWELL, actor, in Leeds, England, on June 13.

GERALDO RIVERA, talk show host, July 4, in New York City.

MICK JAGGER, Rolling Stone, Dartford, England, on July 26.

ROBERT DE NIRO, actor, August 17, in New York City.

MARTIN MULL, comedian and actor, August 18, in Chicago.

LECH WALESA, Polish labor leader, was born in Poland in September 29.

CHEVY CHASE, actor and comedian, October 8, in New York City.

PENNY MARSHALL, actress and director, in New York City, on October 15.

CATHERINE DENEUVE, actress, born Catherine Dorléac, on October 22, in France.

SAM SHEPARD, playwright and actor, November 5, in Fort Sheridan, IL.

MARLO THOMAS, "That Girl!" star, in Detroit, MI, on November 21.

RANDY NEWMAN, singer/songwriter, in Los Angeles, on November 28.

KEITH RICHARDS, Rolling Stone, Kent, England, on December 18.

JOHN DENVER, singer, Roswell, NM, on December 31.

D E A T H S

George Washington Carver, chemist and botanist, born a slave in Mississippi, died in Tuskegee, AL, on January 5, at 79.

Sergei Rachmaninoff, Russian composer, died on March 28, at 70.

Beatrice Webb, British reformer, died on April 30, at 85.

Edsel Ford, son of Henry, president of Ford Motor Company, who had as his namesake the world's most unpopular car, died on May 26, at 49.

Leslie Howard, actor best known as Ashley Wilkes in *Gone With the Wind*, was killed when the plane he was in was shot down by Germans on June 2. He was 50.

Lorenz Hart, lyricist, half of the legendary musical team Rodgers and Hart, died on November 22, at 48.

Beatrix Potter, creator of the Peter Rabbit books, died at 67, on December 22.

43

11

Million-Selling Records of 1943

i'll be home for christmas
(Decca), Bing Crosby

born to lose
(Okeh), Ted Daffan and His Texans

pistol packin' mama
(Okeh), Al Dexter and His Troopers

all or nothing at all
(Columbia), Frank Sinatra with the Harry James Orchestra

besame mucho (kiss me)
(Decca), Jimmy Dorsey and His Orchestra with Kitty Kallen

hit music

The jitterbug continued to be the most popular dance. As part of the fun, the man swung his partner over his back and between his legs!

Crosby had his fifth million-seller in "I'll Be Home for Christmas." The nonsense song of the year was "Pistol Packin' Mama."

Leonard Bernstein, conductor and composer, became the assistant conductor of the New York Philharmonic.

FRANK SINATRA

fiction

1. **the robe**
   by lloyd c. douglas
2. **the valley of decision**
   by marcia davenport
3. **so little time**
   by john p. marquand
4. **a tree grows in brooklyn**
   by betty smith
5. **the human comedy**
   by william saroyan

William Saroyan published his best-known work, *The Human Comedy*. **Herman Hesse** published his masterwork of fiction, *Magister Ludi*. Not surprisingly, war was the subject of two of this year's most successful books. **Richard Tregaskis** wrote about marines in the Pacific in *Guadalcanal Diary*. **Ernie Pyle** completed *Here Is Your War*, a collection of syndicated articles written while he was a war correspondent. English author **H. E. Bates** wrote *How Sleep the Brave*, a popular war novel published under the pseudonym Flying Officer X. **Wendell Willkie**, former presidential contender, looked beyond the chaos of the day to a peaceful future when occupants of earth would live together in harmony in his book *One World*.

In late September, Adolf Hitler's *Mein Kampf* was published in America. It did not top the bestseller lists.

books

The Pulitzer Prize for Literature went to **Upton Sinclair** for *Dragon's Teeth*. **Robert Frost's** *A Witness Tree* won the Pulitzer Prize for Poetry. **Thornton Wilder** won a Pulitzer for Drama for *The Skin of Our Teeth*.

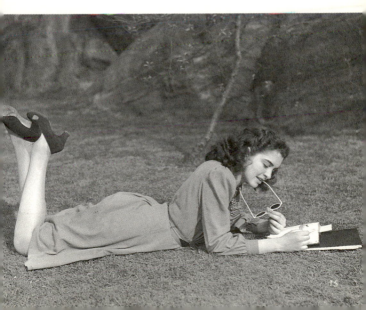

IN BOXING, JAKE LAMOTTA WON AN UNEXPECTED VICTORY OVER THE HIGHLY FAVORED SUGAR RAY ROBINSON.

Yankee great Joe DiMaggio joined the air force as a volunteer.

At West Point, Navy shut out Army in the annual **Army-Navy** game for the 2nd year in a row. The score was 13–0.

In professional football, the Chicago Bears won their 3rd title in 4 years, 41–21, over the Washington Redskins.

In the **Rose Bowl**, Georgia defeated UCLA 9–0. This marked the first Rose Bowl victory by a non-Pacific Coast Conference member since 1937.

sports

In hockey, the Detroit Red Wings won the last 4 games in the Stanley Cup, defeating the Boston Bruins 2–0 to become the National Hockey League champions.

In baseball, the New York Yankees beat the St. Louis Cardinals to win the World Series in 5 games.

COUNT FLEET, RIDDEN BY JOCKEY J. LONGDEN, WON THE KENTUCKY DERBY.

BETTY GRABLE

oscar winners

Best Picture **Casablanca,** Warner
Bros., produced by Hal Wallis

Best Actor **Paul Lukas,**
Watch on the Rhine

Best Actress **Jennifer Jones,**
The Song of Bernadette

Best Supporting Actor **Charles
Coburn,** *The More the Merrier*

Best Supporting Actress **Katina
Paxinou,** *For Whom the Bell Tolls*

Best Original Screenplay **Princess
O'Rourke,** by Norman Krasna

Best Adapted Screenplay
Casablanca, by Julius Epstein,
Philip G. Epstein, and Howard Koch.

Best Director
Michael Curtiz, *Casablanca*

hit movies

1. *This Is the Army*
   Warner Bros. ($8,301,000)

2. *For Whom the Bell Tolls*
   Paramount ($7,100,000)

3. *The Outlaw*
   RKO ($5,075,000)

4. *The Song of Bernadette*
   20th Century-Fox ($5,000,000)

5. *Stage Door Canteen*
   United Artists ($4,330,532)

The all-Black epic *Cabin in the
Sky* scored a popular success
this year, as did canine classic
Lassie Come Home and horror
pic *The Phantom of the Opera.*

movies

TOP 10 BOX-OFFICE STARS
1. Betty Grable
2. Bob Hope
3. Abbott and Costello
4. Bing Crosby
5. Gary Cooper
6. Greer Garson
7. Humphrey Bogart
8. James Cagney
9. Mickey Rooney
10. Clark Gable

There was a marked drop in commercial films
this year. John Ford and Frank Capra were
among several directors making public rela-
tions—some called them propaganda—films
for the Allied governments. John Huston's only
work this year was the narration and direction
of a government-sponsored picture called
Report from the Aleutians.

cars

Gas rationing went into effect on a nationwide basis, a move affecting 27 million cars and 5 million buses and trucks in an effort to conserve gas and rubber tires for the war effort.

The automotive industry this year devoted itself to the war effort, spreading itself to all aspects of defense.

William B. Stout announced development of a "flying automobile" for production after the war.

The Office of Price Administration issued 25 million gas ration books.

Standard outfit for "hepcats" was the **zoot suit**. It featured a long, one-button jacket with broad, padded shoulders, high-waisted trousers that gripped the ankles, a knee-length key chain, and broad-brimmed hat.

It was a year of vivid prints, Tattersall plaids, and checks that disguised wear and tear.

Four styles of suit were in vogue this year: the waistcoat, the bolero, the box jacket, and the hacking jacket.

Very popular were hats that could be wiped clean with a sponge. Quilted or flannel-lined cotton skirts, worsted jackets, and jersey tops were all huge. Lace was used to trim a variety of suits and dresses.

fashion

Most successful blouse designs were bowed at the neck, styled like a jumper, or low-necked for formal occasions. The bare-backed blouse was demure by day, with a suit jacket, and seductive by night without one.

SHOPPING SPREE
Army officer's shirt **$13.50**
Stetson fedora **$20**
Man's suede gloves **$1.98**
British and American woolen overcoats **$63**
Sterling silver cufflinks with colored stones **$2.50**

CAB CALLOWAY

final
factoid

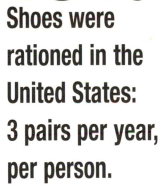

Shoes were rationed in the United States: 3 pairs per year, per person.

archive photos: inside front cover, pages 1, 7, 9, 10, 12, 15, 20, 21, 23, 24, inside back cover

associated press: pages 2, 3, 4, 5, 16

photofest: pages 6, 8, 13, 18

photo research:
alice albert

coordination:
rustyn birch

design:
carol bokuniewicz design
paul ritter